SEACOAST

THE SEASONS OF NEW HAMPSHIRE

Photographs by Bob McGrath

Foreword by Catherine Raynes

SEACOAST, NEW HAMPSHIRE

Seacoast was prepared for publication at Bolton Associates, Inc., San Rafael, CA.
Designer: Joanne Bolton
Text: Palatino
Display: Palatino, Museo Sans Rounded & Bembo

Bob McGrath Photographer L.L.C.
PO Box 932
Rye, NH 03870
www.seacoastbook.com
Printed and bound in China.

ISBN 978-0-615-78033-7

Seacoast –The Seasons of New Hampshire is limited to 5,000 copies.

For the woman who inspires me
To always be the best version of myself.

Eileen, your strength of character,
Your everlasting grace,
Your dedication to our family
And your kind and generous heart
Continue to amaze me
Each and every day.

Emery Farm
Durham

INTRODUCTION

During the spring of 2002 I received a note from a mother of a recent Boston College graduate. In the note she thanked me graciously for the beautiful portraits of her son my studio provided. She sadly explained that her son had lost his life on September 11th and that these photographs had been proudly displayed at her son's memorial service. Experiences in my career have provided great celebration, deep reflection and everything in between, but at a time like this I feel a greater sense of purpose knowing just how deeply photography touches lives.

When a camera's shutter opens, history is made. It is our connection to the past – our memories – and this is what matters the most. Creating this book and my first publication *Rye in Focus,* has been among the most meaningful and rewarding experiences I have had as a photographer.

Traveling throughout the Seacoast Region I am constantly inspired by the beauty of the landscapes and the ever-changing light. I am equally drawn to the people who shape these communities. My most cherished discovery was how quickly I was able to turn strangers into friends simply by asking permission to photograph them, and in most cases these people had crossed my path by pure chance. My goal has always been to respectfully portray people by seeking, through my photographs, to reveal their authentic selves.

I hope you enjoy this book half as much as I enjoyed making it.

BOB MCGRATH

Photographer's note: Photographs were taken with Nikon digital cameras, a D7000 and D3100 using 18mm - 135mm Nikkor Lenses. Images were processed on an Apple iMac Computer utilizing Apple Aperture Software.

FOREWORD

As artists we continually strive to capture moments in time that evoke feelings and memories in our audience. It is an honor when a photograph or painting lives on for generations, serving as a graceful reminder of a place, time or memory.

Within the pages of this photographic journal we are offered a glimpse into a seemingly endless well of profound moments. Through Bob McGrath's lens we are brought into a world of beauty, grit and charm exemplifying the New Hampshire Seacoast. From season to season, we travel from the main roads to off the beaten path, where the nooks and crannies of this region are exposed.

Early on in the writing process I asked people why they live or visit here. While the quality of life, sense of community and proximity to the ocean, mountains and major cities were the consensus, I was most struck by the passion expressed for the area. Bob's images embody this spirit and many yearned for a deeper story to be told. Captivated, I set out to learn more about his experiences and encounters along the way.

The 'true' New Englander was a term that came up often in my conversations with Bob. It is hard to get much truer than the story of *Helen and Bud*–two farmers who live nearly one hundred percent off their land and require very few provisions from the outside world. Helen was raised on dairy farms nearby and has lived to see them go from thriving family businesses to commercial developments and cul-de-sacs. Despite the passage of time and encroachment of the modern world, they hang on to the last vestiges of a profession and lifestyle almost extinct here on the Seacoast. Their incredible work ethic is palpable and their story is awe inspiring as they stay committed to their passion and purpose.

The motorcyclists along the sea wall in Hampton look like any of the myriad bikers seen along the coast, especially in the summer. But strike up a conversation with them and the story goes much deeper. The group belongs to the *Nam Knights of America* and is comprised of US veterans and law enforcement officials. By hosting fundraising events the club's primary mission is to help other veterans who are unable, either physically or financially, to help themselves. Their rough biker appearance in striking contrast to their deep compassion serves as a reminder that things are not always as they appear.

A woman giving out *Free Heartfelt Hugs* at Portsmouth's Market Square Day brightens the festivities. In this technological world, where human contact is sometimes scarce, it is refreshing to meet people putting themselves out there. Bob shared her exuberance was sincere and her sign was genuine – one heartfelt hug had to be received before Bob could take her photo.

Behind the portrait of Doug Scamman is a wonderful story of preservation and dedicated service to the Seacoast region. Doug served thirteen terms as a New Hampshire State Representative and three terms as Speaker of the House and his wife, Stella, served three terms in the Legislature. After stepping down in 2010, the couple turned their energy to their farm. The *Scamman Farm* is an iconic landmark on the Seacoast and if your travels take you down Portsmouth Avenue in Stratham you can't miss it. It sits atop a sweeping hill and in the fall the lawn is strewn with pumpkins, hay bales and corn stalks. The Scammans were rigorous in conserving their 206-acre parcel and, working with the town and the Southeast Land Trust, its long agricultural legacy has been preserved. Their land will forever be protected for farming, forestry, hiking and wildlife habitat.

Turning the pages of this photographic collection you will realize there are many more places of wonder and even more stories to be told. The Seacoast landscape and its people provide a vast, vibrant canvas and through Bob's vision and artistry his photographs serve as a stunning visual catalog of this region captured in time.

CATHERINE RAYNES

Tethered
oil on linen
6" x 8"

AUTUMN

*Autumn is a second spring
when every leaf is a flower.*
—Albert Camus

Wetlands
North Hampton

Applecrest
Hampton Falls

Solitude
Portsmouth

Horses make a landscape look more beautiful.
—ALICE WALKER

Milk Bottles
Stratham

Turn Right
Stratham

University of New Hampshire
Durham

Scamman Farm
Stratham

Buoys
Seabrook

Squamscott River
Exeter

1885
Dover

Town Center
South Hampton

Singing Bridge
Portsmouth

Deadwood
Hampton

Saturday Morning
New Castle

Almost Halftime
Exeter

Kayaks at Sagamore Creek
Portsmouth

Farm Stand
Stratham

In My Footsteps
Rye

The General Store
Newfields

Marsh Art
Rye

Nothing is art if it does not come from nature.

—ANTONI GAUDI

Blue Door
Greenland

Behind the Shed
Stratham

Pond Patterns
Newington

Ready for Winter
Rye

Ford Tractor, Circa 1950's
Stratham

Retired
Seabrook

Shoals Marine
Portsmouth

Nature's Brilliance
Rye

Mid-Morning Light
Stratham

On Track
Greenland

Broken Shutter
Kensington

Halloween Parade
Portsmouth

Natural Palette
Hampton Falls

WINTER

You can't get too much winter in the winter.

—Robert Frost

Snow Day
Rye

Gazebo Mosiac
Exeter

King of the Hill
South Hampton

Snow on Fence
Kensington

Turkey Blizzard
Rye

George's Marina
Dover

Downtown Reflection
Exeter

Street Car
Portsmouth

Town Elections
Exeter

Drifted
Newfields

Two Horses, One Barn
Greenland

Red, White and Blue
North Hampton

Snowy Owl
Rye

The snowy owl rarely migrates this far south but sightings were abundantly reported up and down the Eastern Seaboard. It was believed food scarcity in the arctic was the reason for the massive migration.

Phillips Exeter Academy
Exeter

Library Attic
Newington

Winter Blanket
Rye

The Veterinarian
East Kingston

Bob Marston, DVM founded the first animal hospital in Amesbury, Massachusetts in 1967. His career was spent predominantly on the road caring for horses and cows. Although retired, Bob continues his care and passion for animals on his farm in East Kingston.

Sunday Service
Hampton

Nor'easter
Rye

Raging Seas
Rye

Hope Lynn
Seabrook

Historic Homes
Portsmouth

Gull Frenzy
Rye

... neither snow nor rain nor heat nor gloom of night ...
Hampton

Boxes in Buckets
Seabrook

Driveway Duty
North Hampton

Night Shift
North Hampton

Meandering Stream
North Hampton

Just a Dusting
North Hampton

Dusk
Hampton Falls

Ice Fishing Shacks
Stratham

Steam rising from sugar houses often signals spring's arrival. Each year, the New Hampshire maple industry produces close to 90,000 gallons of maple syrup.

Maple Sugaring
Stratham

Tree by the Sea
New Castle

Plastered
North Hampton

Wagon Hill Farm
Durham

49

SPRING

*Spring is the time of year
when it is summer in the sun
and winter in the shade.*
— CHARLES DICKENS

Through the Curtain
Exeter

Tulips
North Hampton

April 16?!
Greenland

Socked In
Portsmouth

The Big Thaw
New Castle

It's not what you look at that matters, it's what you see.

—HENRY DAVID THOREAU

Honk for Assistance
East Kingston

Burrows Brookside Audubon
South Hampton

Downtown, New England Style
Kensington

A Return from Sea
Portsmouth

Patterns in Contrast
New Castle

3 Kings
Portsmouth

Spring Essentials
Newmarket

Locks of Love
Portsmouth

Rugby Match
North Hampton

Marching Tubas
Portsmouth

Squamscot Old Fashion Beverages has been run by the Conner family since it was first established in 1863. They are the last independent bottler in New Hampshire.

Soda by the Bottle
Newfields

Marelli's Market is celebrating its 100th anniversary. The market is still a family-owned and operated business and is run by the founders' sons and granddaughters.

Family Tradition
Hampton

Orange Bob
New Castle

Tug Boats
Portsmouth

A Working Seaport
Portsmouth

61

Anchor's Away
Portsmouth

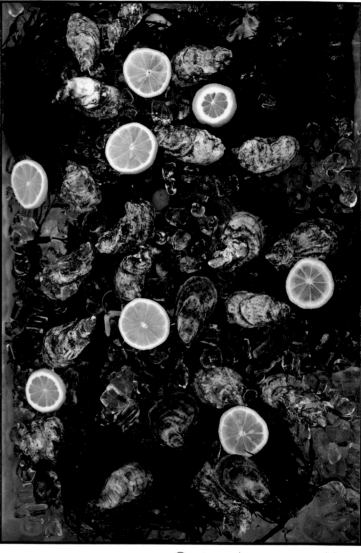

Oysters, Lemons and Ice
Portsmouth

Hilton Park
Dover

Finally Spring
South Hampton

Tranquility
Durham

Great Island Common
New Castle

Riding Solo
Hampton

Water Jugs
Rye

Free Heartfelt Hugs
Portsmouth

Yellow Dump Truck
North Hampton

Little Free Library
Hampton

Table for Two
Portsmouth

Bear Right
Hampton Falls

Daisy Salute
Rye

You will never do anything in this world without courage.
It is the greatest quality of the mind next to honor.

—ARISTOTLE

A Moment of Silence
Rye

Forever in Our Hearts
Rye

We Honor, We Respect
Rye

SUMMER

*Summertime is always the best
of what might be.*
— Charles Bowden

Heading to Sea
New Castle

Time to Chill
Rye

Cocheco Falls
Dover

Fourth of July
Rye

'I don't even know you.'
Hampton

Beach Day
Hampton

Some of the best memories
are made in flip-flops.
—Kellie Elmore

Summer Lights
Portsmouth

Take Off
North Hampton

Soccer Camp
Durham

Victory Park Motors
North Hampton

A Work Day for Grampa
Hampton

Memorial Bridge
Portsmouth

Stratham Fair
Stratham

Waiting for Her Forever Home
Stratham

'We are their voice.'
—ASPCA

JD in Charge at Strawbery Banke
Portsmouth

Morning Mist
Rye

Surfing USA
Hampton

Fairy Houses
Portsmouth

UNH Dairy Bar
Durham

Kaeleigh's Wedding Day
Rye

Farmers' Market
Durham

Fresh Beets
Exeter

Cliffside
Star Island

Helen and Bud
Rye

Sisters by the Surf
Rye

Oyster River
Durham

Sky Fire
Seabrook

Heroic, Lost at Sea
Hampton

Fuller Gardens
North Hampton

9:45 a.m.
Newmarket

Homebound
Star Island

'To Protect and to Serve'
Dover

A hero is somebody who voluntarily walks into the unknown.

—TOM HANKS

A Firefighter, A Marine
Exeter

Sand Expressions
Hampton

UFO Festival
Exeter

The Arrival
Star Island

Welcome to planet earth.

—Mark Goddard

Blue Cooler
Hampton

Nam Knights of America
Hampton

Approaching Storm
Rye

Docked
Star Island

Mayellen's Rainbow
North Hampton

Legacy in Hand
Hampton

Revisiting History
Portsmouth

Full Bloom
Portsmouth

The Bell
Star Island

Bridge Jumping
Rye

Waves Wanted
Hampton

Three Little Pigs
Hampton

Reflections of the Past
Hampton

'North Hampton Forever'
North Hampton

Window Box
Newmarket

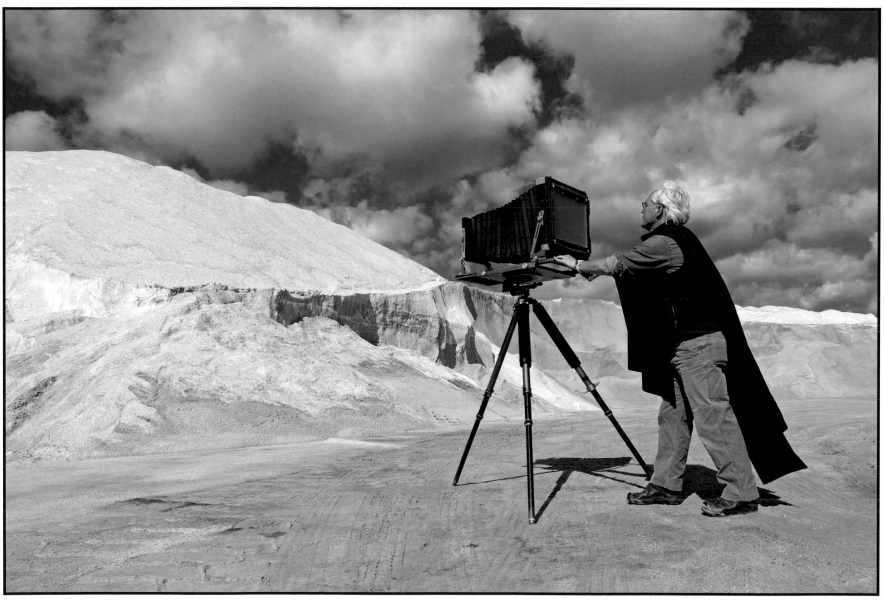

Carl, 11x14 Camera & Salt Piles
Portsmouth

A true photograph need not be explained,
nor can it be contained in words.
—ANSEL ADAMS

The Strip
Hampton

First Place
Hampton

Seaside Dinner
Hampton

Eight Tomatoes
Kensington

Tendercrop Farm at the Red Barn
Dover

One Afternoon
Seabrook

Kennedy Rocker
Star Island

Hampton Beach Seafood Festival
Hampton

Silhouettes
Seabrook

Ideal Evening
Hampton

A Season to Remember
Seabrook

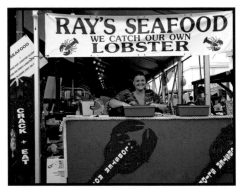

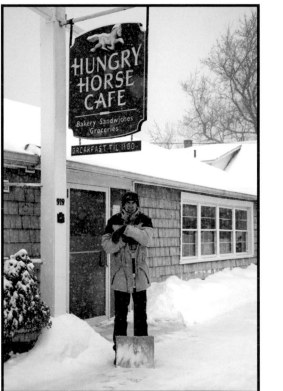

Seacoast — The Seasons of New Hampshire would not be complete without expressing my gratitude to the following contributors:

- ⚓ *Roberta and Jack McGrath – Without my parents' encouragement and support I would have never taken the path that has brought me to here.*
- ⚓ *Catherine Raynes – Her writings and editing collaborations have brought life to my photographs. Her passion is infectious and her commitment to the arts is extraordinary.*
- ⚓ *Joanne Bolton – Joanne's enthusiasm and talent for producing great books has earned her the title 'Superwoman of Print.' I am tremendously grateful to have her on my team.*
- ⚓ *Jim Williams – A true mentor and friend, Jim with his heart of gold, is a master of wisdom and a sultan of words.*
- ⚓ *Mike Peltier – Relying on Mike has always been an easy decision. His integrity and wit make for a great combination of friend and business colleague.*
- ⚓ *New Hampshire Chronicle, Yankee Magazine, New Hampshire Magazine and The Portsmouth Herald – Their support and praise have made the difference in the transformation of a self-published book into a beloved keepsake.*

Finally, my heartfelt 'thank you' to all who have embraced my photographic endeavors. Your kind words and moving letters have been a driving force behind this book.